MACHINES MADE SIMPLE

Levers

Written by Kirsty Holmes

KidHaven PUBLISHING

Published in 2026 by
KidHaven Publishing, an Imprint of
Greenhaven Publishing, LLC
2544 Clinton St., Buffalo, NY 14224

Written by: Kirsty Holmes
Edited by: Elise Carraway
Designed by: Amelia Harris

Cataloging-in-Publication Data
Names: Holmes, Kirsty.
Title: Levers / Kirsty Holmes.
Description: Buffalo, NY : KidHaven Publishing, 2026. | Series: Machines made simple | Includes glossary and index.
Identifiers: ISBN 9781534550728 (pbk.) | ISBN 9781534550735 (library bound) | ISBN 9781534550742 (ebook)
Subjects: LCSH: Levers--Juvenile literature. | Simple machines--Juvenile literature.
Classification: LCC TJ147.H65 2026 | DDC 621.8'11--dc23

Manufactured in the United States of America

CPSIA compliance information: Batch #CSKH26
For further information contact Greenhaven Publishing LLC at 1-844-317-7404.

Please visit our website, www.greenhavenpublishing.com.
For a free color catalog of all our high-quality books, call toll free 1-844-317-7404 or fax 1-844-317-7405.

Find us on

Image Credits

All images are courtesy of Shutterstock.com, unless otherwise stated. Cover – ewapee, MNI, Dja65, StockSmartStart, Vlarvixofs. Recurring images – Onica Alexandru Sergiu. 2–3 – Heavypong, New Africa. 4–5 – Smileus, Stephane Bidouze. 6–7 – Gorodenkoff, Ljupco Smokovski. 8–9 – fiyixiang, a_v_d, Ljupco Smokovski, Serhiy Stakhnyk, Master1305, HummingBean, Juan Roballo. 10–11 – vectortank88, jufitapamilu. 12–13 – Chiyacat, New Africa. 14–15 – fs_typesetting, Unkas Photo, Mark S Johnson. 16–17 – Ljupco Smokovski, Vadzim Mashkou. 18–19 – mang gigit, chaossart. 20–21 – ARTpok, New Africa. 22–23 – DukiPh, EAKARAT BUANOI, Dolores M. Harvey, Savanevich Viktar, VectorMine.

Contents

WORDS THAT LOOK LIKE THIS CAN BE FOUND IN THE GLOSSARY ON PAGE 24.

Marvelous Machinery

Your everyday life is probably filled with machines. Machines can be very big and complicated, like an excavator. They often have lots of moving parts and can do difficult jobs.

Did you know that machines can also be really simple? Some machines have very few moving parts and do simple jobs. Even a stick you use to dig in the soil is a type of simple machine.

SIMPLE MACHINES DO SIMPLE JOBS.

What Is a Machine?

Machines help us do all sorts of jobs. These jobs can be simple or complicated. A spade does the simple job of digging a hole. A computer can do complicated jobs, such as figuring out the way to the moon!

SEVERAL SIMPLE MACHINES CAN WORK TOGETHER TO CREATE A COMPLICATED MACHINE.

Simple machines use forces to get their jobs done. A force, such as a push or a pull, changes the speed or direction of an object. For example, when you push someone on a swing, you use a force.

A BIGGER PUSH SENDS YOU SWINGING HIGHER!

What Is a Lever?

A lever is a simple machine. Levers can be used to move things using a push or pull force. Levers can help lift and move heavy things or make things go up and down. Scissors, wheelbarrows, and seesaws all use levers.

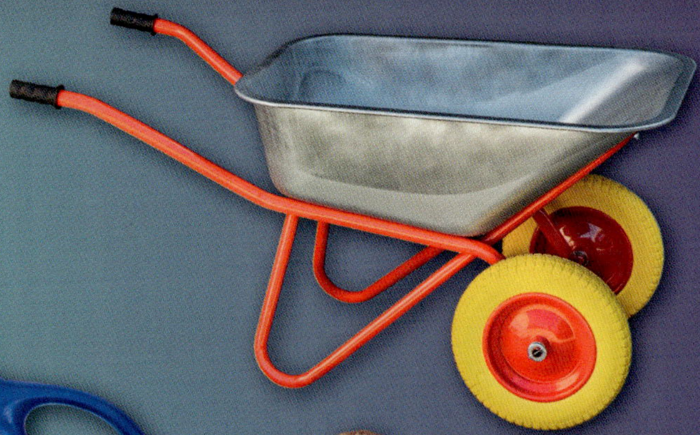

These simple machines all use levers. Do you know what they are all used for?

1
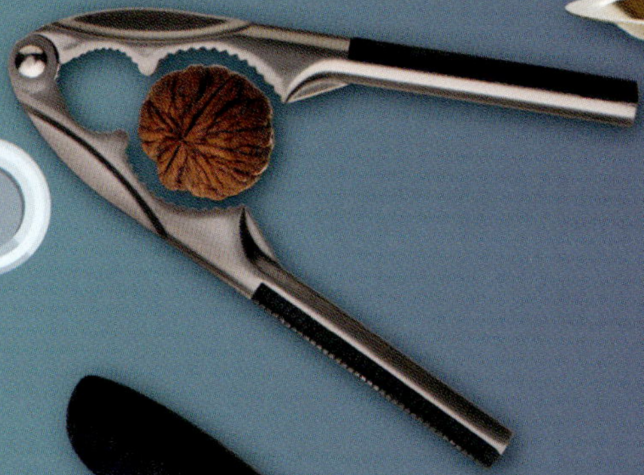

2

3

4
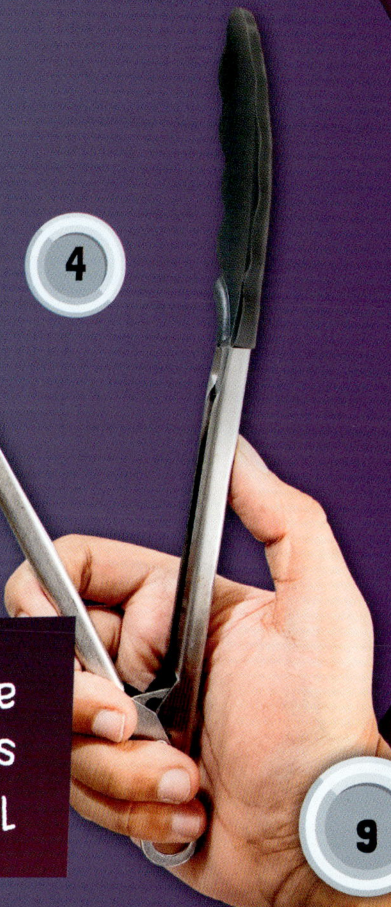

1. Nutcracker (breaking shells) 2. Balance scale (measuring weight) 3. Paddle (moving a boat) 4. Tongs (picking things up)

Parts of a Lever

All simple levers have a load, a fulcrum, and a beam. You use effort to move the load.

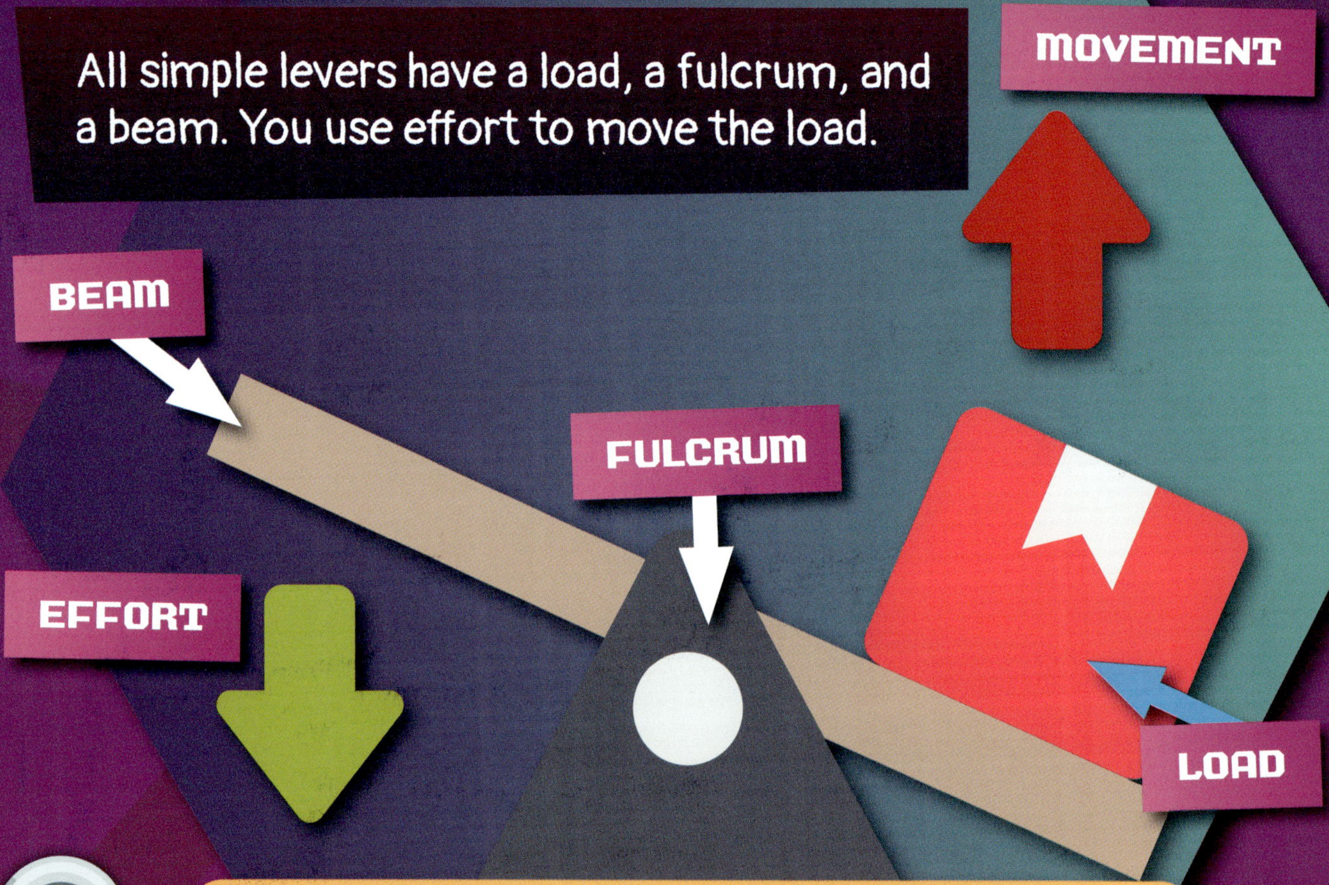

The load is the thing you want to move. The beam is a stiff rod or plank that holds the load. Pushing or pulling one end moves the other end the other way. The beam moves against a fixed point called the fulcrum.

Changing Forces

A lever, like any simple machine, changes the forces used to move a load. The input force is called the effort. The lever takes the effort and changes it, making it bigger or smaller.

A lever can change the input force into a much bigger output force. This means levers can be used to move loads that a person could not move on their own. This is known as mechanical advantage.

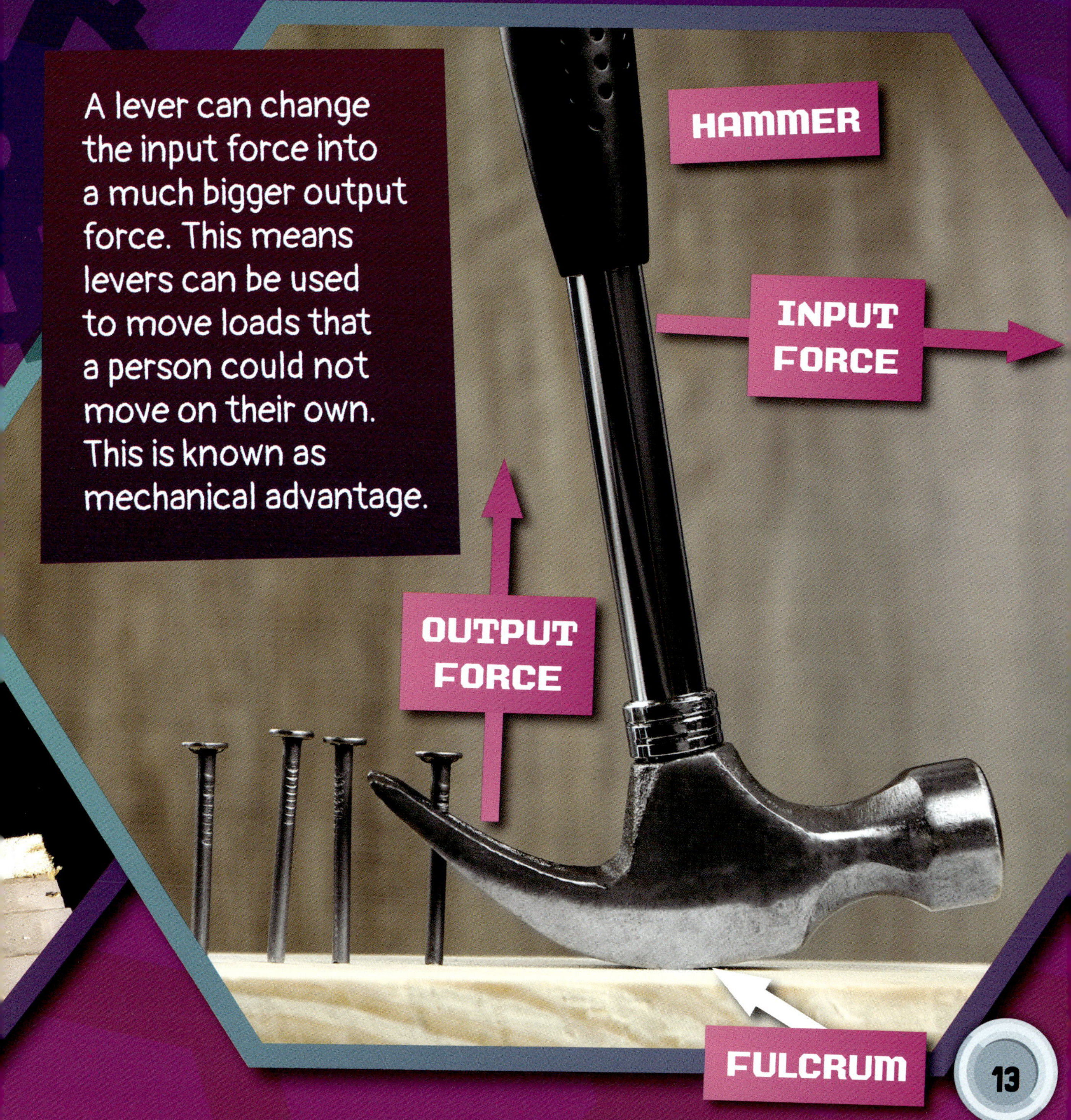

Different Types of Levers

There are three main types of levers. In each type, the parts are in a different order. The position of the fulcrum affects the amount of effort you need to use to lift the load.

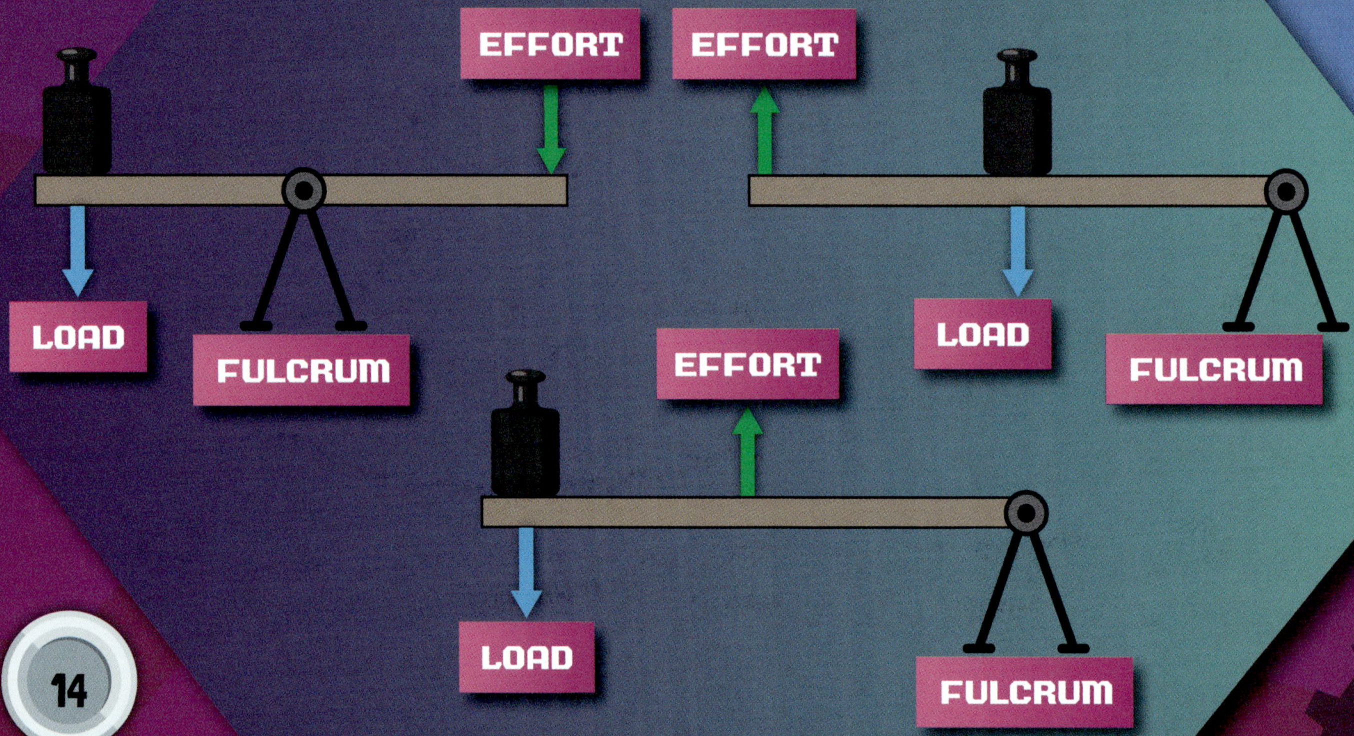

Some levers help move loads that are heavier than a person could move by themselves. Other levers help move things more precisely.

A CRANE IS A BIG LEVER FOR MOVING HEAVY LOADS...

...AND TWEEZERS USE LEVERS TO MOVE TINY THINGS!

First Class Levers

A first class lever has the fulcrum between the effort and the load. When the fulcrum is closer to the load, less effort is needed to move the load.

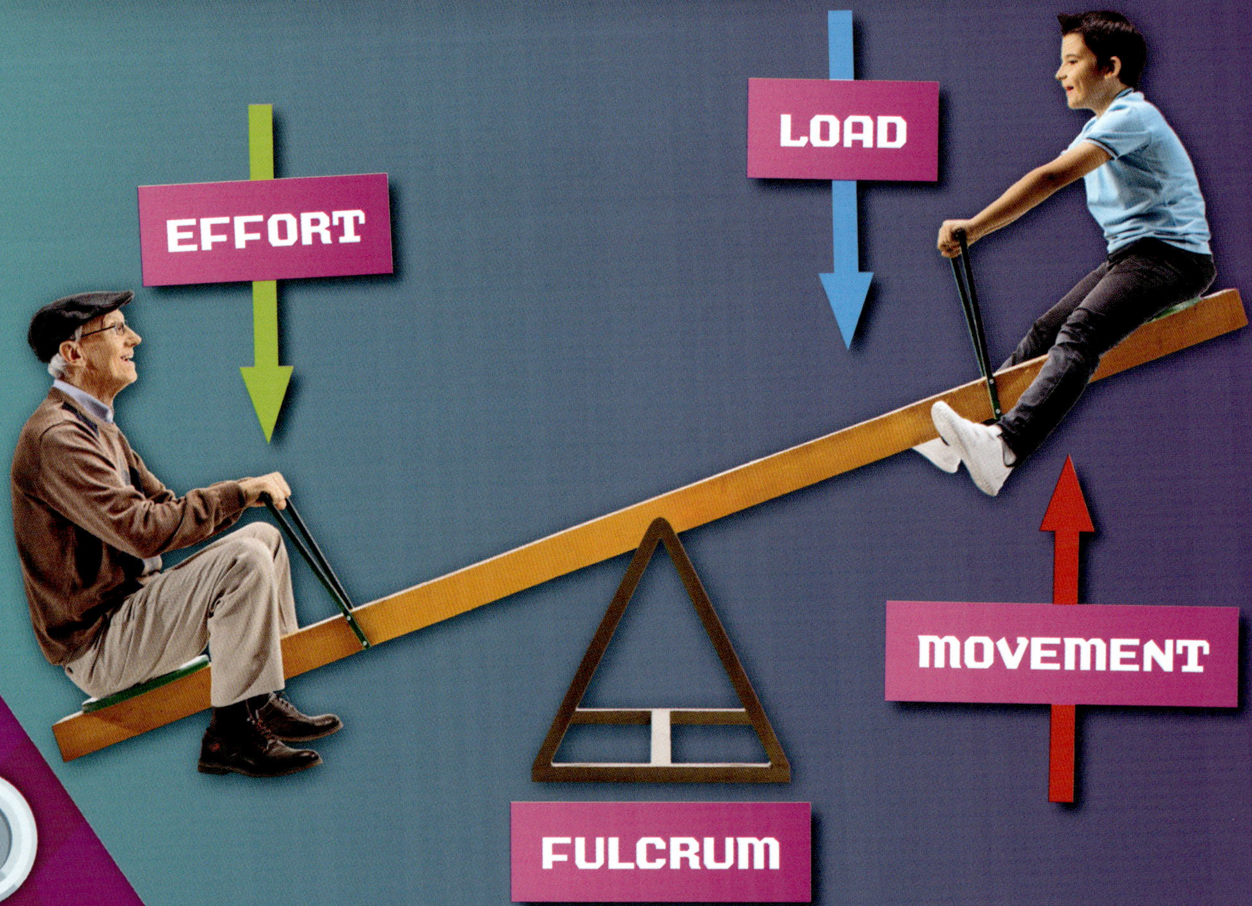

Examples of First Class Levers

- Seesaw
- Crowbar
- Light switch

SCISSORS ARE TWO FIRST CLASS LEVERS JOINED AT THE FULCRUM.

Second Class Levers

Second class levers have the load between the effort and the fulcrum. Just like first class levers, the closer the load is to the fulcrum, the easier it will be to move it.

A WHEELBARROW USES A SECOND CLASS LEVER. IT HELPS BUILDERS CARRY HEAVY LOADS.

Examples of Second Class Levers

- Stapler
- Door
- Nutcracker

DOING A PUSH-UP TURNS YOUR BODY INTO A SECOND CLASS LEVER!

Third Class Levers

Third class levers have the fulcrum at one end, the effort in the middle, and the load at the other end. If the fulcrum is closer to the effort, the load will move farther.

A HAMMER IS A THIRD CLASS LEVER. THE MOVEMENT HELPS THIS MAN SWING THE HEAVY HAMMER HEAD.

Examples of Third Class Levers

- Fishing pole
- Garden rake
- Broom

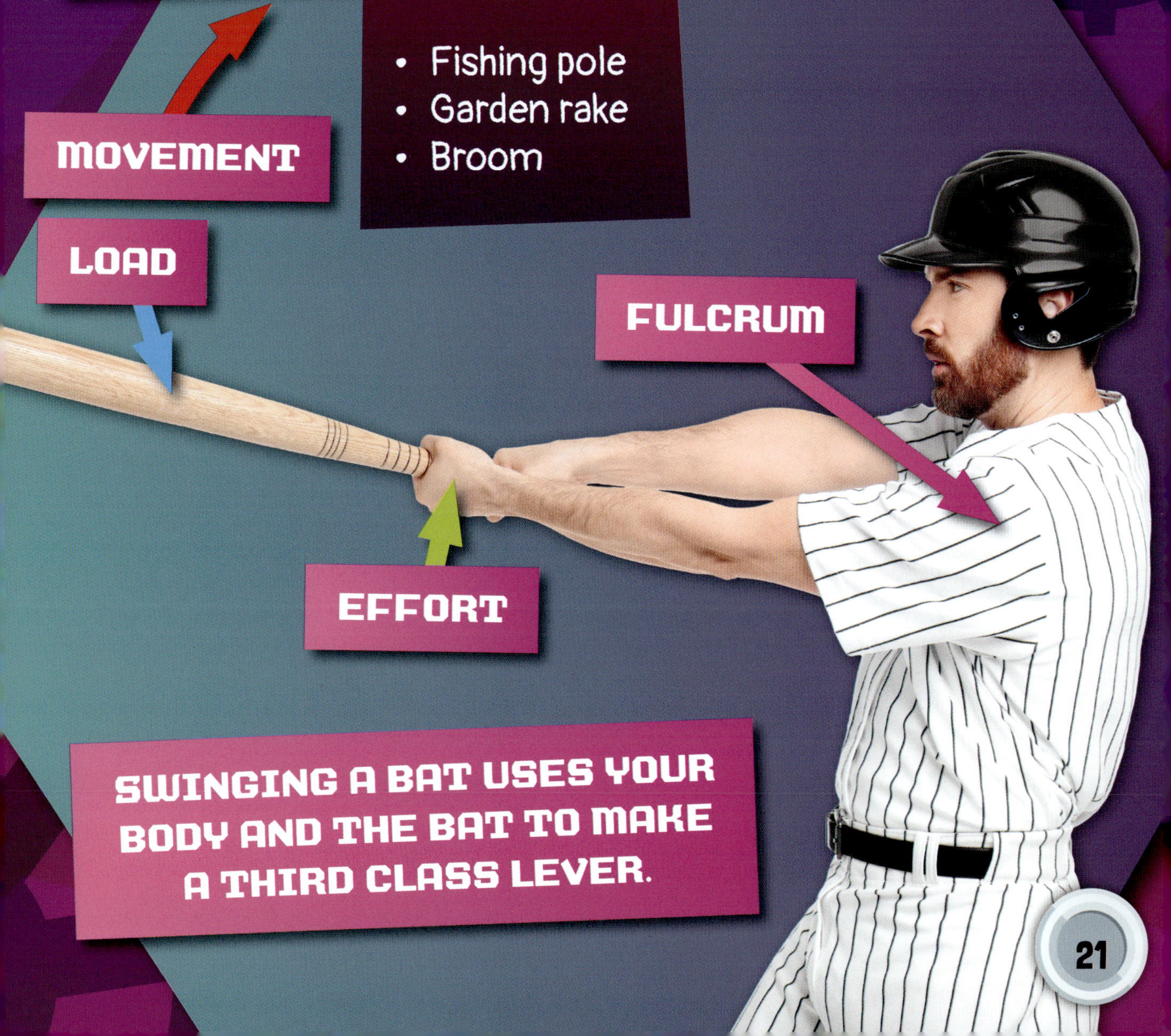

SWINGING A BAT USES YOUR BODY AND THE BAT TO MAKE A THIRD CLASS LEVER.

Super Simple

Levers are simple machines, but they are used for so many things. How many levers can you find...

...IN THE KITCHEN?

...AT SCHOOL?

...AT THE PLAYGROUND?

...ON A BICYCLE?

Did you know your body is also full of levers? How many levers can you think of in your body?

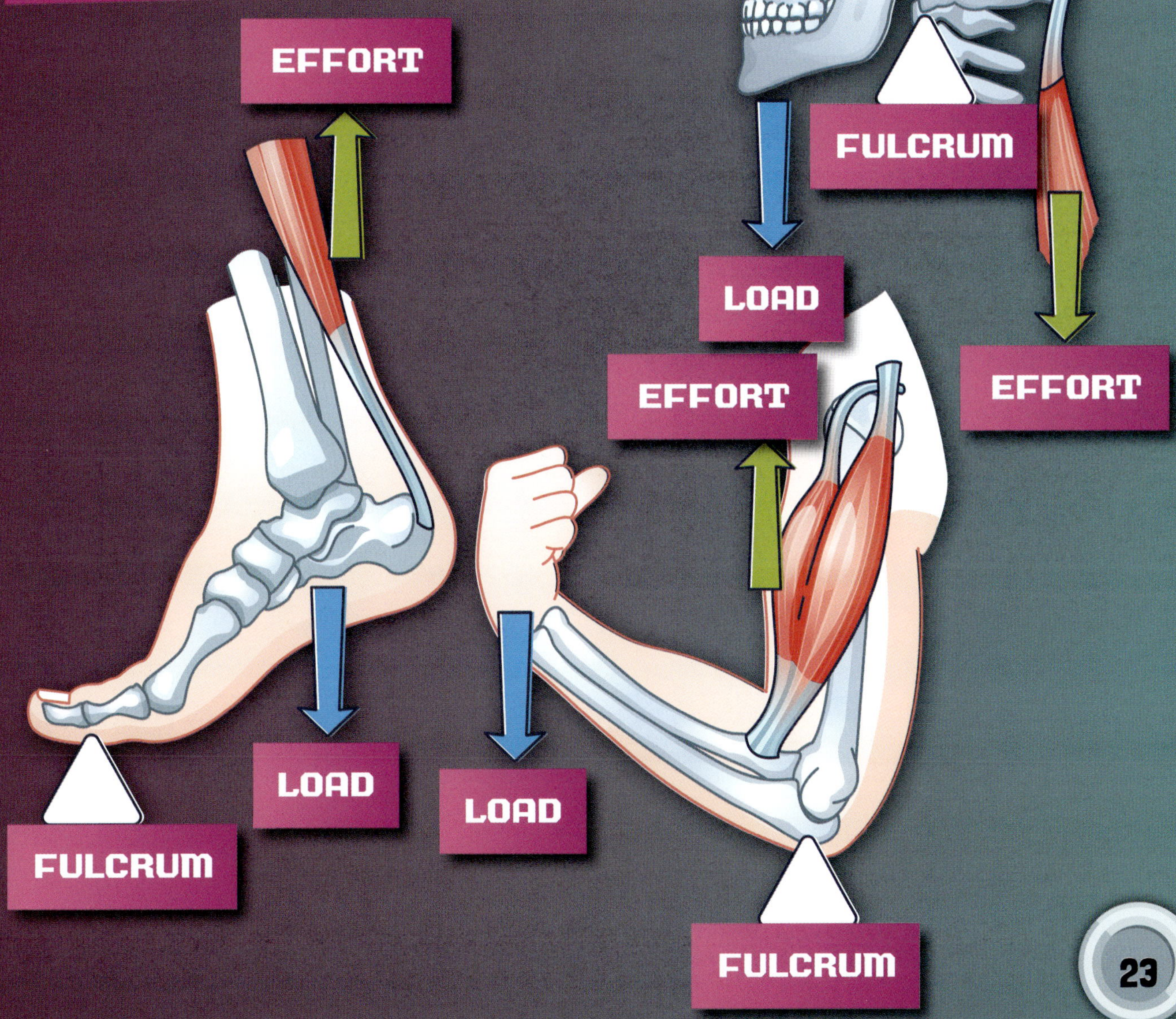

Glossary

precisely	exactly
rod	a thin, straight bar, especially made from wood or metal

Index